# shabbat can be

illustrated by yuri salzman

# shabbat can be

raymond a. zwerin / audrey friedman marcus

union of american hebrew congregations

This series of holiday books for young children
dedicated to Mildred and Matthew H. Ross

is made possible by

The Blum Family Publication Fund


*Max and the late Ida*
*Helene and the late Sidney*

Library of Congress Catalog Card Number: 78-70669
ISBN 0-8074-0023-8

*Manufactured in the United States of America*

2 3 4 5 6 7 8 9

To our children and our children's children,
for whom we hope the Shabbat can be.

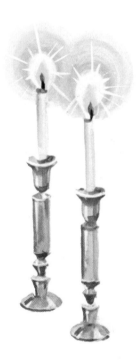

SHABBAT can be different from any other day.
Shabbat can be many things.
Let's see what Shabbat can be for you.

SHABBAT can be
your mother's eyes as sh

ights the Sabbath candles.

SHABBAT can be
singing Kiddush and tasting a sip of sweet wine.

**SHABBAT** can be
biting into a piece of soft, golden chalah.

SHABBAT can be
loving hands upon your head.

SHABBAT can be
you saying amen lots of times.

SHABBAT can be
the special way your stomach feels
when you see and smell your favorite foods.

SHABBAT can be
singing zemirot
with people you love.

SHABBAT can be
thank You, God, for making me me.

**SHABBAT** can be
hearing Rabbi tell a story.

**SHABBAT can be warm in synagogue with your family and your friends.**

**SHABBAT can be resting.**

**SHABBAT** can be
a queen who spends the day with you.

SHABBAT can be
a special day for Jews near you
and Jews far away.

SHABBAT can be
when everyone is fair
to everyone else.

**SHABBAT can be
reading a wonderful Jewish book.**

**SHABBAT can be
like standing on top of a mountain.**

SHABBAT can be
when everyone is free.

**SHABBAT** can be feeling rich without a penny in your pocket.

**SHABBAT can be
your happiest dreams.**

SHABBAT can be
a joy so big that it takes two of you to hold it.

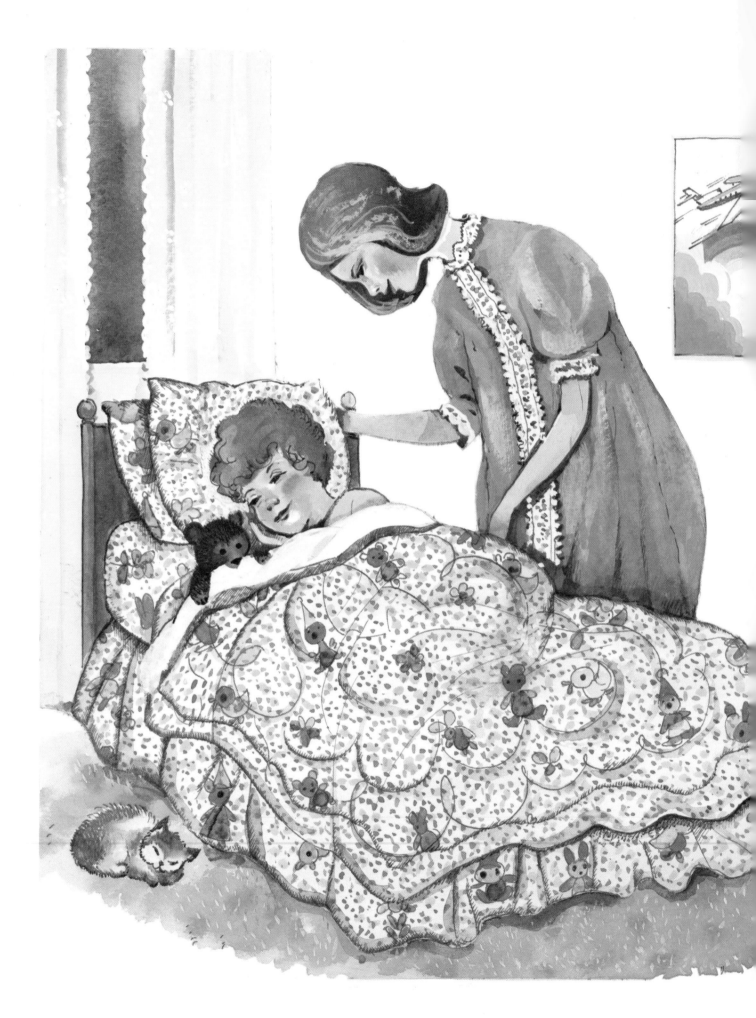

**SHABBAT** can be
the nice way you feel just before you fall asleep.

SHABBAT can be
many things.
What can it be for you?

## About the Authors

Among their occupations and many activities, RAYMOND A. ZWERIN is the founding rabbi of Temple Sinai in Denver, Colorado, author of the UAHC text *For One Another,* and AUDREY FRIEDMAN MARCUS is the editor of *Alternatives* magazine and past director of education of Temple Micah in Denver. Whether separately or together—as partners in their own publishing company, Alternatives in Religious Education, Inc.—they are known and respected for their innovative approach to Jewish education. Their numerous books and games are the delight of Jewish children everywhere.

And *Shabbat Can Be* is their latest, joyful celebration of Jewish tradition.

## About the Artist

YURI SALZMAN, a permanent resident of the United States since 1976, immigrated from the Soviet Union where he studied at the Moscow Art School and the Moscow Poligraphic Institute. Some of the 90 or more books he has illustrated have been exhibited in Russia, Yugoslavia, Egypt, Syria, and East Germany.

*Shabbat Can Be* is Mr. Salzman's first commissioned work in the United States and he is now busy illustrating children's books for Harper & Row and Holt, Rinehart & Winston.

## Some Very Special People

June Marshall, Sandra Bernstein, Dr. Jack Horowitz, Judy Hoffman, Rabbi Daniel B. Syme, Rabbi Steven M. Reuben, Ralph Davis, Gerry Gould

A publication of the

**UAHC-CCAR**
Joint Commission on Jewish Education